For Sophia Julia Goldman

—

A FEIWEL AND FRIENDS BOOK
An imprint of Macmillan Publishing Group, LLC
120 Broadway, New York, NY 10271 • mackids.com

Our books may be purchased in bulk for promotional, educational, or business use.
Please contact your local bookseller or the Macmillan Corporate and Premium Sales Department
at (800) 221-7945 ext. 5442 or by email at MacmillanSpecialMarkets@macmillan.com.

Library of Congress Cataloging-in-Publication Data is available.

First edition, 2022

Book design by Mike Burroughs
The artwork was drawn traditionally and colored digitally.
Feiwel and Friends logo designed by Filomena Tuosto
Printed in China by RR Donnelley Asia Printing Solutions Ltd., Dongguan City, Guangdong Province

ISBN 978-1-250-13859-0 (hardcover)

1 3 5 7 9 10 8 6 4 2

Madame Alexander

THE CREATOR OF THE
ICONIC AMERICAN DOLL

"Dolls live in the hearts of children . . . that is where they truly come alive."
—Madame Alexander

Susan Goldman Rubin   Illustrated by Sarah Dvojack

Feiwel and Friends
New York

More than one hundred years ago, a little girl named
Beatrice Alexander looked out her window to the bustle
below. Beatrice's parents had come across the ocean to America
and settled in New York City. Many families like theirs had
moved into a neighborhood called the Lower East Side, where
the buildings overflowed with people.

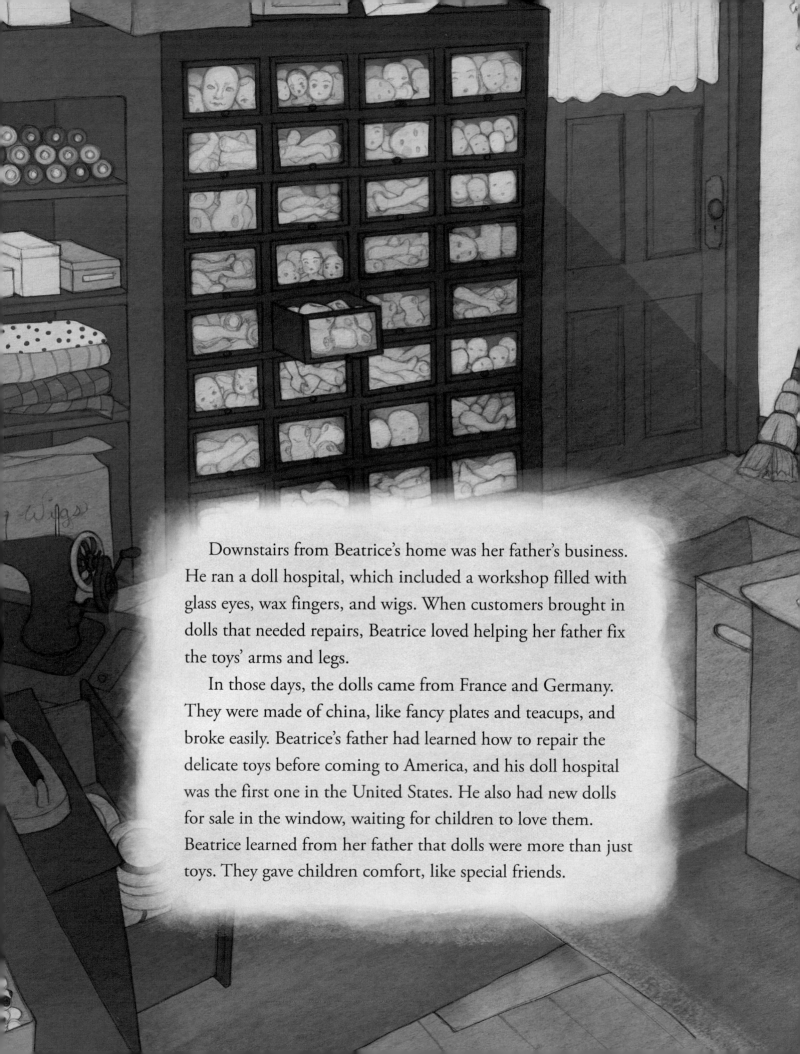

Downstairs from Beatrice's home was her father's business. He ran a doll hospital, which included a workshop filled with glass eyes, wax fingers, and wigs. When customers brought in dolls that needed repairs, Beatrice loved helping her father fix the toys' arms and legs.

In those days, the dolls came from France and Germany. They were made of china, like fancy plates and teacups, and broke easily. Beatrice's father had learned how to repair the delicate toys before coming to America, and his doll hospital was the first one in the United States. He also had new dolls for sale in the window, waiting for children to love them. Beatrice learned from her father that dolls were more than just toys. They gave children comfort, like special friends.

Every day after school, Beatrice stayed in the doll hospital
while her three younger sisters played tag and hopscotch outside.
Her father needed her to patch up the patients' chipped noses and
cracked faces. She washed the dirty faces of dolls, then watched her
father paint their eyebrows and lips. Beatrice wanted to paint, too.

Carriages coming from uptown would pull up to the busy hospital, and wealthy ladies wearing huge hats with feathers and little girls wearing velvet coats would sweep into the shop. They would bring their broken dolls all the way to the M. Alexander Doll Hospital because it was known as the best in New York. Beatrice longed to wear velvet and feathers, too.

The little girls were often crying and terribly sad because their dolls were hurt.

"We'll take good care of your doll," said Beatrice to every unhappy child. "I promise my sisters and I will keep her company till she's better."

Some days she and her sisters invited friends to come play
with the dolls. The neighbors loved visiting the hospital because
most children on Grand Street didn't have extra money for toys.
Beatrice led the girls in singing get-well songs to the dolls.

In the space behind their little house, her parents had planted roses and daisies in a secret garden. There, Beatrice would read poems and her favorite library books to the broken dolls.

Ideas swirled through her head. What if she made dolls like characters in the books to act out the stories? Beatrice imagined what the dolls would look like, what they would wear. Their dresses. Shoes. Even their underwear!

Every Friday at sundown, Beatrice's mother lit the *Shabbos* candles and blessed them to welcome the Sabbath. And Beatrice's father went to *shul* (synagogue) to hear the *magid* (the traveling storyteller) after the service. When he came home, he told the day's lesson to Beatrice: "Do good works and give to others." The words stayed with her, and she never forgot them.

Most nights, her mother washed doll wigs to get them ready for repairs while Beatrice did her homework. She loved to read, but arithmetic was her best subject.

Many other girls on the Lower East Side at that time left school when they were twelve years old to take jobs in factories and earn money for their families. But Beatrice's parents insisted she keep up with her good grades. "Someday the world will hear of her," boasted her father.

One night, loud banging at the door
woke Beatrice's family.

A man rushed in carrying his little girl
and her doll. The child was bawling.

"Doctor!" shouted the man. "*Please* fix my daughter's doll.
My daughter is sick, and she won't take her medicine without her doll."

"Of course," said Beatrice's father, even though it was the middle of the night.

The doll's head was shattered into bits like a smashed teacup. How could they ever put it back together?

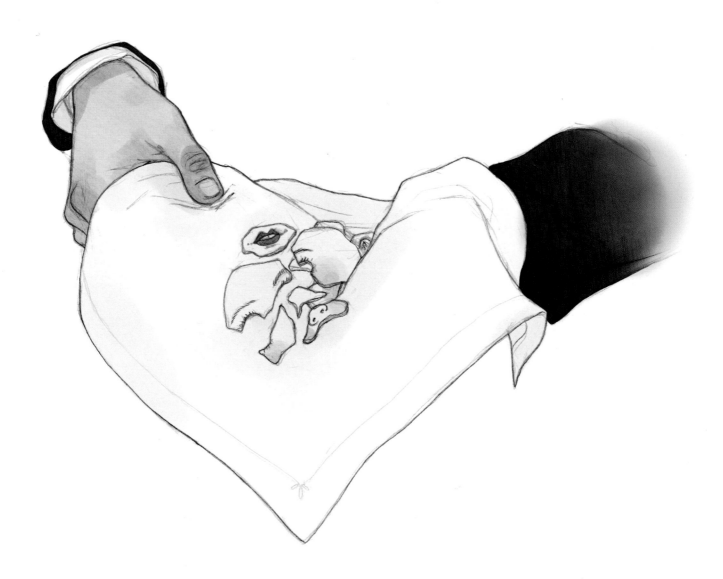

Beatrice's father trusted her to help him with this difficult job.

Side by side at the workbench, they found the right pieces, fit them into place, glued them, and let them dry.

Glue spotted Beatrice's nightgown and stuck to
her fingers. Her eyes burned from searching hard for
the right bits. Her back hurt from hunching over
and she wanted to stretch, but she didn't dare stop.

At last, by morning, the job was done. The little girl hugged the doll as the man hugged Beatrice's father. "You saved my child," he said.

"My Beatrice helped, too," said her father. And Beatrice beamed.

Yawning, Beatrice went upstairs to get ready for school. She remembered the child's tears of misery. She had seen that children need dolls to love, cuddle, talk to, and share secrets with.

Someday, she thought, *I will make dolls that don't break so children will never be unhappy.*

When she was thirteen, Beatrice went to a public
high school for girls.

Not only was she good at reading and arithmetic,
but also drawing, painting, and modeling clay. She
loved working with her hands.

Walking home in the crowded streets, past peddlers
selling pickles and pretzels, she daydreamed. What if she
became a real artist?

When she was sixteen, she had a chance to study sculpting in Paris! She won a scholarship for her outstanding artwork, and it would pay for everything. Beatrice burst into the house to tell her parents.

But they couldn't let her go. The bank where they had put their savings had lost all of the family's money, and they needed her help at home.

Beatrice was overwhelmed with disappointment. Yet, she agreed.
She knew her own desires would have to wait. She stayed home. She
took a job to earn money for her family as she continued school. But
she never stopped dreaming.

Soon, Beatrice met a young man named Philip Behrman. When she graduated from high school and turned eighteen, she married Philip, and the couple lived near her parents and sisters.

Not long after, the Great War broke out. It was impossible to get
new dolls or even parts of dolls from countries across the ocean.

The doll hospital shelves stood empty. Customers stopped coming.
The family business was in trouble, and Beatrice worried.
"We have no dolls," said her father. "But children still need them."
Beatrice knew he was right. She thought and thought.

Then Beatrice came up with an idea. "We will make our own, with cloth so the dolls won't break."

"But what will the dolls look like?" asked her sisters.

Beatrice remembered the posters she had seen. "The Red Cross nurses who take care of injured soldiers," she said. By hand, she sewed the first white nurse uniform, blue cape, and tiny white cap. And her sisters copied hers. They all stuffed the dolls with wood shavings and cotton.

People loved the nurse dolls. They bought them and wanted more.

Now, the family had some money again.

Now, Beatrice was a doll maker!

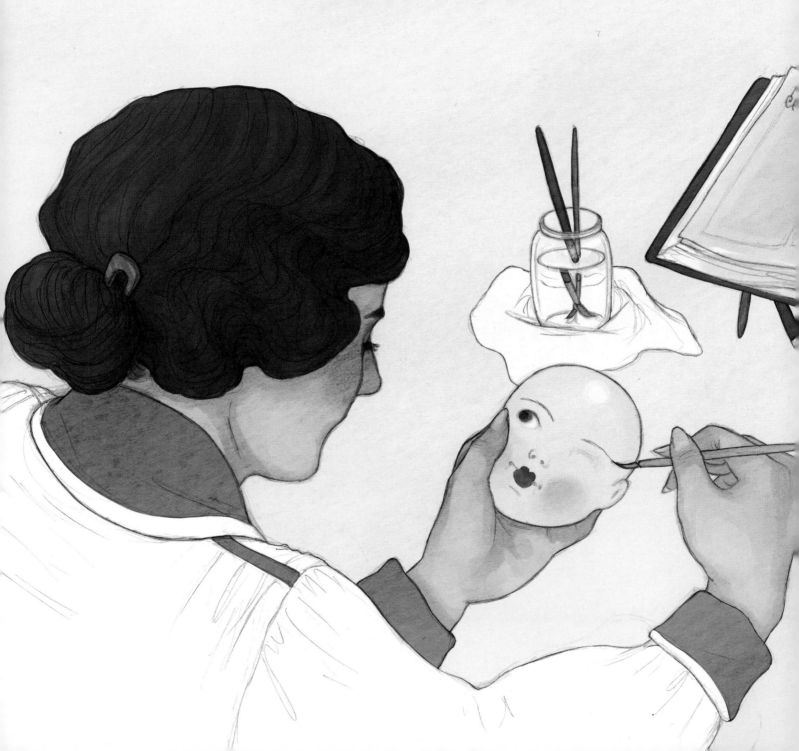

As the war went on, she kept working at her office and then helped her family put dolls together. Making dolls delighted Beatrice, and as she worked, an idea popped into her head. She dashed to the library and flipped through her favorite books to learn what girls wore long ago.

Beatrice made a rag doll that looked like an old-fashioned girl in a pretty handsewn dress. But the doll's face was flat. So Beatrice used some buckram—wet cotton soaked with paste. She put the material over a little cereal bowl and shaped a new face with her hands to make the cheeks puff out. She painted the mouth, eyes, and eyebrows the way her father used to do on china. She attached yarn for the doll's hair. When her family saw what she was doing, they helped make more dolls just like Beatrice's model. By the end of the day, they had made twelve rag dolls.

Beatrice put the dolls in the window, and people
bought them. She glowed with pride.

Before long, Beatrice and her husband had a baby named Mildred.

Having a daughter reminded her of when she and her sisters took care of the dolls like mothers. It gave her a new idea. She sculpted a baby doll that looked like her daughter, Mildred.

To earn money, neighbors joined the family, working late at
night. In the morning, customers jammed the shop and bought
all the baby dolls.

The war was over now. Things were changing, and Beatrice
made changes, too. She needed a bigger workplace and more
helpers. She had to sell more dolls at a higher price in more places
than just their own doll hospital. There was only one place to go.

Bravely, she wrapped up one of the baby dolls and took it uptown to the very best toy store in New York City: FAO Schwarz. Wealthy women and men went there to buy toys for their children.

Beatrice was scared. What if they didn't want to do business with a Jewish woman from the Lower East Side?

She held her breath as the head of FAO Schwarz unwrapped the doll. "Adorable!" he exclaimed, and then ordered dozens for the store.

Beatrice was thrilled. Now she had her own business at a time when not many women were bosses in the workplace.

With her husband's help and a full staff, Beatrice was free to imagine all kinds of dolls and fancy clothes. She could even have a doll hospital like her father's for mending dear old dolls, and her new dolls would go to children who would play with and love them.

Word spread about Beatrice's dolls. A reporter wrote a story about her and gave her a grand new name: Madame Alexander.

Over the years, Madame Alexander made smart decisions to grow her business. She eventually opened a factory with offices, showrooms, and a staff of fifteen hundred workers. Madame Alexander kept running the company even as she faced many hardships. But she was tough and clever and never gave up.

She was the head of her own company all her life, overseeing every detail, from the elegant doll box design to the smallest brushstroke on an eyelash so her dolls would look real.

Madame Alexander would stand in the showroom proudly gazing at her beautiful, unbreakable creations displayed on the shelves. Ballerina dolls, baby dolls, grown-up dolls in gowns and jewels . . . More dolls than she could have ever imagined back in the kitchen above her father's doll hospital. Dolls that looked like all sorts of people in America and the countries their families had come from. "American dolls for American children."

More About MADAME ALEXANDER

1.

Madame Alexander was born on March 9, 1895, in Brooklyn, New York. She was named Bertha but later changed her name to Beatrice. Her father had died before she was born, and her mother, Hannah Pepper, an Austrian-born Jewish immigrant from Russia, had remarried Maurice Alexander, a fellow Jewish immigrant from Russia. Separately, they had fled pogroms in Russia. At that time, the late-nineteenth century, antisemitic mobs and Czar Alexander III's Cossacks viciously attacked Jewish people. They burned homes, looted stores, and killed thousands of Jews. Millions of Eastern Europeans escaped to the United States.

In their new homeland, Hannah and Maurice started a family. They had three more daughters: Rose, Florence, and Jean. Beatrice adored Maurice and always thought of him as her true father.

During the same year that Beatrice was born, Maurice Alexander established a doll hospital at 405 Grand Street on the Lower East Side of New York. According to Beatrice and journalist Krystyna Poray Goddu, it was the first doll hospital in the United States, and it was marked by a blue sign with a white cross. Of all the Alexander girls, Beatrice was the one who loved helping their father in the doll hospital.

After Beatrice married, had a baby, and produced her first successful cloth dolls, she borrowed money from the bank and established the Alexander Doll Company in 1923. Few businesswomen founded companies in those days, but Beatrice hungered to have a career. She worked six days a week making dolls. Her staff of sixteen included her sisters and neighbors on Grand Street. As the business thrived, she rented a studio and became Madame Alexander.

There are many versions of how she acquired her professional name. In an interview, Beatrice said that a doll salesman told her she looked French and suggested she call herself Madame. Journalist Mary Margaret McBride used the aristocratic title when she wrote an article about Beatrice that boosted sales.

In the mid-1920s, Beatrice moved her growing company to a storefront and factory space in Manhattan. She found a better material for making unbreakable doll bodies, papier-mâché mixed with resin and sawdust. However, Beatrice faced crises that almost forced her to give up: the Spanish flu pandemic, a flood in her factory, and the Great Depression, the fallout after banks and businesses failed in 1929. People hardly had enough money for food, much less children's toys. Beatrice needed to come up with an idea for affordable, appealing dolls. Inspired by literature, she produced a cloth *Alice's Adventures* doll, then a set of *Little Women* dolls. A movie version of *Little Women*

came out at that time and was a huge hit, and the dolls sold extremely well. Thanks to Beatrice's clever idea, the Alexander Doll Company stayed in business. Beatrice went on to invent "sleep eyes," dolls' eyes that opened and closed; upper eyelashes made of human hair; rooted hair; and a walking doll. She made boy dolls, too.

During World War II, despite a shortage of materials, Beatrice still produced well-dressed dolls. She remembered how her mother had crocheted edges on petticoats, and she did the same for her dolls. Beatrice knew that little girls loved dressing their dolls, and she wanted even the undergarments to be pretty.

After the war, when plastic and fine fabrics became available, Beatrice exploded with ideas. She created every category—from baby dolls and play dolls that looked like little girls, to storybook characters and commemorative dolls such as the Dionne quintuplets in Canada and Princess Elizabeth in England. When Beatrice's daughter got married and had a baby girl named Wendy, she introduced the Wendy Ann doll. The plastic mold for Wendy's face was used for millions of different dolls.

Then, in 1955, four years before Barbie, Beatrice presented Cissy, a full-figured female fashion doll in high heels. She understood that little girls sometimes liked to play grown-up. Beatrice also wanted children to learn about different cultures in the U.S. and the world. She designed international dolls wearing traditional clothing. Her dolls were known for their detailed painting, wigs, and gorgeous attire.

By 1957, Beatrice ran three factories. She combined the factories and relocated them in a single building in the Harlem section of Manhattan, and re-created a doll hospital there. In the 1980s, the company released more than one million dolls each year. Women who treasured their Madame Alexander dolls formed fan clubs. The Brooklyn Children's Museum and the Smithsonian placed Madame Alexander dolls in their collections. FAO Schwarz named Beatrice the "First Lady of Dolls." She was one of the most successful businesswomen of her time.

2.

3.

But she always remembered her father's lesson of giving to others. Beatrice generously contributed to institutions such as Brandeis University, Harvard University, the American Friends of the Hebrew University, and the Anti-Defamation League. She was also one of the founders of the Women's League for Israel.

On October 3, 1990, Madame Alexander died at the age of ninety-five. But the Alexander Doll Company carried on her legacy of producing beautiful, unbreakable dolls that children could play with and cherish.

BIBLIOGRAPHY

4.

BOOKS

Bial, Raymond. *Tenement: Immigrant Life on the Lower East Side.* Boston: Houghton Mifflin Company, 2002.

Diner, Hasia R. *Lower East Side Memories: A Jewish Place in America.* Princeton and Oxfordshire: Princeton University Press, 2000.

Finnegan, Stephanie. *Madame Alexander Dolls: An American Legend.* New York: Alexander Doll Company, Inc. and Portfolio Press Corporation, 1999.

Goddu, Krystyna Poray. *Dollmakers and Their Stories: Women Who Changed the World of Play.* New York: Henry Holt and Company, 2004.

Hopkinson, Deborah. *Shutting Out the Sky: Life in the Tenements of New York 1880–1924.* New York: Orchard Books/an Imprint of Scholastic Inc., 2003.

Howe, Irving, and Kenneth Libo. *How We Lived: A Documentary History of Immigrant Jews in America 1880–1930.* New York: Richard Marek Publishers, 1979.

Horwitz, Joshua. *Doll Hospital.* New York: Pantheon Books, 1983.

Irwin, Julia F. *Making the World Safe: The American Red Cross and a Nation's Humanitarian Awakening.* New York: Oxford University Press, 2013.

McDonough, Yona Zeldis. *The Doll Shop Downstairs.* New York: Puffin Books, an Imprint of Penguin Group Inc., 2009.

INTERVIEWS

Transcript of an interview with Beatrice Alexander conducted by Rose Miller, March 16, 1982. Series: American Jewish Women of Achievement. William E. Wiener Oral History Library of The American Jewish Committee. New York Public Library—American Jewish Committee Oral History Collection. Research call number: **P(Oral Histories, Box 339 no.2)

ARTICLES

Cushman, Sandi. "They're Real Dolls, and You Can't Beat That These Days," *Daily News* (New York, New York), November 5, 1974, page 245.

Marian, Ellias. "Madame Alexander: American Dolls for American Children." *Playthings*, July 1, 1984.

Scott, Dorey Finn. "Madame Alexander: A Living Doll," *Palm Beach Daily News*, March 7, 1982.

ARTICLES ONLINE

Altman, Julie. "Beatrice Alexander 1895–1990," Jewish Women's Archive, February 2009.

Brody, Seymour "Sy." "'Madame' Beatrice Alexander: The First Lady of Dolls," *Jewish Heroes and Heroines in America from 1900 to WWII.*

Finnegan, Stephanie. "Bertha Alexander—A Glorious Legacy," *Dolls* magazine, October 1, 2004.

Ingall, Marjorie. "The Woman Behind the Dolls," *Tablet*, May 7, 2013.

Jarvis, Gale. "The Doll Authority: An Interview with Gale Jarvis, President, The Madame Alexander Doll Company, LLC," *Lifestyle*, October 2014.

Trucco, Terry. "Where to Find It; Where Dolls Go When They're Sick," *New York Times* print archive, December 6, 1990, Section C, page 2.

"A doll should stimulate a child's imagination," she once said.
"A doll can undoubtedly become a child's best friend."